WITH MY BANJO ON MY KNEE

THE
MINSTREL SONGS
OF
STEPHEN FOSTER

*arranged for
minstrel banjo by*

DANIEL PARTNER

historical notes by

EDWIN J. SIMS

CENTERSTREAM

arrangements copyright © 2008 by Daniel Partner
text copyright © 2008 by Edwin J. Sims
ISBN 13: 978-1-57424-229-4
ISBN 10: 1-57424-229-6

Centerstream Publishing, LLC
P.O. Box 17878 · Anaheim Hills, CA 92817
714.779.9390 · Centerstrm@aol.com
www.centerstream-usa.com

Production and design by
CAPITAL A PUBLICATIONS, LLC
1429 East Thirteenth Avenue
Spokane, WA 99202
www.capitala.net

TABLE OF CONTENTS & TRACK LIST

Edwin J. Sims supplies the percussion accompaniment to Daniel Partner's banjo performance of the musical arrangements in this book. Mr. Sims plays the bone castanets, or simply, the bones. This was the most common rhythm instrument of the antebellum minstrels, and one of the most ancient of musical instruments. The minstrels adopted the bones to lend validity to their southern slave impersonations, despite the fact that the instrument came to America from Europe, not Africa.

The bones are made from either animal bones or various types of wood. One pair of the flat, slightly curved sticks are held between the fingers of each hand. A motion of the wrist causes one bone to strike the other, generating a distinct clacking sound. As Stephen Foster wrote in "Ring, Ring De Banjo!," *De ladies nebber weary Wid the Rattle ob the bones!*

Mr. Partner plays a reproduction pre-Civil War banjo, which is fretless, with a goatskin head and sheep-gut strings, as pictured on the back cover of this book. Please note: If the listener finds a discrepancy between the recorded and printed version of a song, the printed version takes precedent.

STEPHEN FOSTER & THE BANJO
A MUSICAL TRANSFORMATION

American popular music was forever changed on September 11, 1847, at Andrew's Eagle Ice Cream Saloon in Pittsburgh, Pennsylvania. There, a certain song was performed in public for the first time. This song, like a new national anthem (Emerson 1997, 123), catapulted our country to the forefront of popular music in the Western World. The song is "Oh! Susanna," its writer is Stephen C. Foster, and its main character is a banjo player.

It can be argued that no song published in the United States has ever been more popular than "Oh! Susanna." One hundred and sixty years ago, the tune was heard in all corners of the country. Today, when one sings a few bars of this song in those same regions, faces light up in recognition. We agree with one of Mr. Foster's biographers who wrote that his "songs are an American institution, a cultural export from antebellum days to the present, and one of the largest individual contributions to cultural export from the United States to the world at large" (Saunders 1990, xiii).

In the decade that preceded the publication of "Oh! Susanna," the music of the blackface minstrel stage had taken America by storm. Northern musicians blended the melodies of Anglo-Celtic music with the rhythms of the music of enslaved black Americans. The result was wholly unique and unquestionably all-American. At the core of this music was the banjo, which developed from a musical instrument introduced to the Americas some two centuries earlier by enslaved Africans. Well aware of the banjo's popularity, the songwriter cast a banjo player as the protagonist in his famous song who, in our imagination, has been searching for Susanna and playing the banjo from Alabama to Louisiana ever since.

Stephen Foster had a hand in producing nearly 300 musical works; songs written for, and performed in churches, Sunday schools, patriotic rallies, middle-class parlors, and big-city theaters. The most enduring of these are the songs he wrote for the blackface minstrel stage where they were played on the banjo. On the tide of these, his most popular songs, Foster rose to become the best-known songwriter of his time, and the banjo was firmly established in mainstream American music.

With this book we hope to provide an understanding of how Stephen Foster's minstrel songs were played on the banjo in the mid-nineteenth century and, to the best of our ability, help the reader reproduce the original sound of that music. Historical notes provide insight into the meaning and milieu of these songs. We are not under the illusion, however, that the passing of 160 years does not affect our interpretation of Mr. Foster's music. In order to control this, we've limited ourselves to the use of the earliest sheet music for each of the sixteen songs herein, including the original lyrics. Plus, we play reproduction minstrel-style banjos, and have learned our playing technique from the banjo tutors of the antebellum era, especially *Briggs' Banjo Instructor* (1855). The minstrel songs of Stephen Foster presented in this book are arranged to reflect the style transmitted by the authors of those books.

DANIEL PARTNER   EDWIN J. SIMS
Coos Bay, Oregon   Sacramento, California

THE AMERICAN SONGWRITER
STEPHEN C. FOSTER

Stephen C. Foster's birth in Lawrenceville, Pennsylvania came on the fiftieth anniversary of the signing of the Declaration of Independence. On that July 4, 1826, the fragile union faced formidable political and social problems, and was already on the road toward the fiery trial that would refine it into the nation we know today. The Civil War is such a colossal event in the national psyche that it cloaks the decades that led to its outbreak. In those years, Stephen Foster gave musical expression to the American experience that pierces that cloak and resonates to this day.

Foster's family grappled with financial problems as their youngest child grew up. Still, young Stephen was raised in a life decidedly more privileged than that familiar to most Americans of the day. He did not excel in academic studies but did take to music at an early age. Foster's older brother, Morrison, later reported, "Sister Ann Eliza had a number of musical instruments, among the rest a guitar. When he was two years old he would lay this guitar on the floor and pick harmonies from its strings" (Foster 1932, 31).

While still young, Foster mastered the flute and, more importantly, the piano on which he later composed his melodies. In 1844, the Philadelphia music publisher George Willig published the sixteen-year-old lad's "Open Thy Lattice Love." Foster published many such parlor songs during his career. But, in the mid-1840s, he, like countless Americans, was being mightily attracted by the magnetic new music of the blackface minstrels.

While the Ethiopian Serenaders and Christy's Minstrels were packing theaters in New York City, Stephen Foster toiled as an accountant in his brother's Cincinnati shipping concern. But his fertile mind was not completely focused on bookkeeping. Within this quiet man lay the inspiration to do something no American had done before. He was about to become this country's first professional songwriter.

> The decision to give all of his time to music was made . . . because, when Foster came of age, it was apparent that he could write songs that would be successful commercially. With that proof in his hand [the sheet music of "Oh! Susanna"], he had an argument to convince his friends and family that he could earn as good a living in music as others could in the accepted channels of commerce—perhaps better (Howard 1962, 134).

Soon, because songwriting was no longer his hobby, each new song had to be popular in order to sell. Stephen Foster's first major success, "Oh! Susanna," is the song most associated with his name. Though it was written for big-city minstrel troupes, the song was frequently heard as far away as the California gold fields, and was reportedly played as British troops marched off to fight the Crimean War in 1854:

> About a mile out, the head of the blue column came in sight, and to the strains of "Cheer, boys! Cheer!" and "Oh, Susanna, don't you cry for me," the gallant lads, with their red and white pennons fluttering gaily from the lance shafts, rode in through the streets thronged with onlookers, who cheered them to the echo, and dismounted near the quay somewhere about ten o'clock (Brighton 2004, 31).

"Oh! Susanna" was America's first outright smash hit song, its unofficial national anthem, and coveted cargo at the beginning of our cultural exportation to the world. In the two years following the song's public release, sixteen different publishers released it in thirty different arrangements with very little money or recognition going to Foster (Emerson 1997, 139). Nonetheless, the importance of "Oh! Susanna" to Foster was more than monetary. Through it, he realized that he could make a living as a songwriter, and because of this, the world of music would soon change significantly. In those days, the popularity of a song was judged not by how many times it was performed, but by the number of sheet music copies purchased. Before Foster and "Oh! Susanna," sheet music publishers considered performers most important to the selling of their product. Foster's advent gave songwriters equality with performers, and eventually brought them preeminence.

So, on the strength of "Susanna's" success, Stephen Foster took the bold step to make his living solely by songwriting. He moved to Pittsburgh, Pennsylvania to be close to his family, and concentrated on composing music for the wildly popular minstrel troupes for which the music-buying public clamored. "The country was in the grip of the minstrel craze, and this genuinely American institution made an amazing appeal to all classes of the American people. New melodies for the minstrels, which appeared almost as rapidly as they could be printed and copyrighted, were quickly seized upon by the eager public, tried on the piano and other available instruments, and whistled on the streets" (Wittke 1968, 58).

From 1848 to 1853, Foster became America's best-known songwriter because of his minstrel music, which "united resonant poetic images with memorable melodies" (Saunders 1990, xxxviii), and so elevated the standard of minstrelsy. This popularity gave him confidence to move away from using the popular Negro dialect and the word *nigga* in his lyrics. In Standard English, his descriptive lyrics alone gave the typical slave's voice of the minstrel song greater force. Even the covers on his sheet music reflected this change: Foster's early songs were labeled "Ethiopian Melodies." Later ones were called "Plantation Melodies." Foster wrote romantic parlor ballads during this time, but they did not profit him as much as did his minstrel songs.

The reason for Foster's turn from the Negro dialect is unknown. Some authors claim (without evidence from primary sources) that this was because of the composer's increasing awareness of the plight of American slaves and the need for social change. This is doubtful. Despite his musical genius, Foster was a man of the times, and so not particularly enlightened regarding racial equality. Still, his Plantation Melodies humanized the slaves as no songs had done before. They convey the impression that, when it came to home and family, enslaved blacks harbored the same emotions as did free whites.

Changes in Foster's personal life at this time mirrored those of his professional life. He was married in 1850 and his only child was born the next year. Soon after, he moved with his family from Pittsburgh to New Jersey to be closer to his publishers. His popularity and income were on the rise, but hard times lay in wait.

It may never be known why, at the height of his popularity in 1854, Foster quit writing minstrel songs. However, this coincided with problems in his personal life—that year he separated from his wife and daughter. Though he would intermittently reunite with his family, this, combined with increasing alcoholism and decreasing income, took its toll on the man.

Foster briefly returned to minstrel music in 1860 and 1861, and even though minstrelsy was as popular as ever, he could not regain his previous status. At this time, his family left him for good. When the American Civil War began in 1861, he joined his fellow songwriters in producing patriotic songs. However, these, along with his parlor ballads, generated little success for him.

Stephen Foster died alone on January 13, 1864, in New York's Bellevue Hospital, yet his work abides to this day. One hundred and sixty-one years after the publication of his first song, on February 13, 2005, a compilation of his music performed by various contemporary musicians titled "Beautiful Dreamer: The Songs of Stephen Foster" won a Grammy Award.

Due to their healthy vitality, Foster's songs have stood the tests of time in peace and war, and have emerged as fresh and strong and ever-young. They have become, not only a part of the American heritage, but of the world's heritage. If music can achieve for itself immortality, then the simple melodies of the modest Pittsburgh composer will be heard for all time (Morneweck II 1944, 600).

DREAMING OF MINSTRELS
STEPHEN FOSTER
& POPULAR CULTURE

The fifteen songs in this book are among the most popular of Stephen Foster's catalog. He wrote them to be performed by the blackface minstrels of his day—northern, Caucasian males who typically played songs that combined elements of the Anglo-Celtic tradition and the music of American slaves. This unique music was the core of the mid-nineteenth century minstrel show, and was the first purely American popular entertainment. Minstrel music was so dominant that it supplanted the traditional music of the slaves, took the country by storm, and became America's first entertainment export. From the 1840s to the 1890s, minstrelsy was the nation's most popular form of entertainment.

> Everywhere it played, minstrelsy seemed to have a magnetic, almost hypnotic, impact on its audiences. "A minstrel show came to town, and I thought of nothing else for weeks," Ben Cotton recalled of the first time he saw minstrels in the 1840's in Pawtucket, Rhode Island. George Thatcher, later a minstrel star, had comparable feelings when as a boy in Baltimore he saw his first show. "I found myself dreaming of minstrels; I would awake with an imaginary tambourine in my hand, and rub my face with my hands to see if I was blacked up . . . the dream of my life was to see or speak to a performer." After Dave Wambold, later a minstrel tenor, attended his first minstrel show in Newark, New Jersey, his parents could not keep him in school because "he was wont to play truant and get up minstrel performances among his companions." Similarly, Joel Chandler Harris, Stephen Foster, M. B. Leavitt, and Al G. Field—all later important in American popular culture—were stage-struck boys who played minstrelsy in their youth. Minstrels had truly captured the imagination of the nation (Toll 1974, 33).

Prior to the era of minstrelsy, America lacked a clear national identity. Therefore, its professional entertainment was imported from Europe. Victory in the War of 1812 precipitated a nationalism that, thirty years later, caused Americans to eagerly accept the newly developed indigenous music of the minstrel stage on which Stephen Foster's music claimed the limelight. At this time, Americans in the north were fascinated with the idea of slaves and Southern plantation culture although these were far removed from their lives. Made-up in blackface and dressed in stylized slave's clothing, the so-called Ethiopian delineators employed a black dialect, took to the stage with their banjos, and satisfied their countrymen's curiosity with an ersatz expression of plantation life. In 1852, a reader of the *Musical Times* wrote, "The Negro Melodists are the only species of National Amusement that we can boast of. They sing the songs of the Plantation Slaves of the South, dance their Plantation jigs, and imitate the language of the real Virginia Negro" (Lawrence 1995, 313).

Just as a minstrel always performed in blackface, he invariably appeared with a banjo. West Africans, captured by slave traders, brought the banjo's prototype to the Americas. This developed into the instrument that lent the required African authenticity to minstrelsy. It was ubiquitous in the minstrels' performances, the lyrics of their songs, and even the illustrations on their sheet music. The basic lineup of an antebellum min-

Ferrotype of Stephen Foster taken between 1859 and 1860. Foster Hall Collection, Center for American Music, University of Pittsburgh Library System.

typical images, has caused people to shun the study of minstrelsy and the performance of minstrel music. However, the dismissal of minstrelsy as purely racist entertainment damages American history. We are indebted to musicologist William J. Mahar for this explanation:

> Blackface minstrelsy was a complex commercial and cultural enterprise. The sum of its many parts added up to more than the commercialized exploitation of racial imitation or the commodification of ethnic or racial envy and white superiority. From the contents of the shows to the organization of the programs, from the allegedly authentic "delineations" of African Americans to the representation of women, and from the curious banjo songs of the 1840s to the sophisticated opera parodies of the 1850s, antebellum minstrelsy established a now familiar pattern in American popular culture. Musical material borrowed from the cultural periphery establishes itself as a viable commercial product and develops into a respectable mainstream entertainment purged of any features that would complicate unduly the audience's perceptions of the need (or lack thereof) for radical changes in American attitudes toward race, gender, and class (Mahar 1999, 329).

Minstrel songwriters and performers offered audiences wonderful entertainment while creating powerful social satire and burlesque. Certainly white racism was included in this mix. However, this was found in nearly all aspects of antebellum life. Foster and other songwriters often subverted racist ideologies by incorporating antislavery arguments and sympathetic portrayals of slavery's victims into their music. "The reining tonality of the minstrel show in its popular years was of course upbeat. But there was a gaping sore at the heart of all this cheer. The early work of Stephen Foster (a sort of one-man research and development team) alone contained the main elements of sentimentalized plantation distress on which most minstrel companies capitalized forthwith" (Lott 1995, 187). Many songwriters also criticized and burlesqued the upper class, European entertainers, American politicians, religion, the Victorian moral code, and a host of other issues all the while rein-

strel troupe included a banjo, fiddle, tambourine, and bones. An additional banjo, fiddle, or other instrument was sometimes added. The fiddle played co-melody, harmony, or rhythm and was secondary to the banjo, which was the lead or melodic instrument. Bones and tambourines were the most common percussion instruments although triangle, jawbone, and other instruments were also used. Since many minstrel tunes were originally meant to accompany a solo dancer, we believe their tempos were slower than what is common among old-time or bluegrass string bands today. Also, our experience has taught us that their loquacious lyrics often demand a slower tempo in order to be sung with clarity.

The themes of the songs of the blackface minstrels describe the experiences of African-American slaves as imagined by European-American songwriters. This fact, together with their use of the word *darkey* and *nigger,* and many stereo-

forcing society's attitudes toward blacks, women, immigrants, and other minorities.

Was there thoughtful social purpose in the themes and characters that Mr. Foster and his contemporaries incorporated in their songs? Yes, there was. This is present in many songs simply because it helped sell them to the middle class consumer. The public attended minstrel shows to hear the songs they enjoyed. Likewise, people bought sheet music of their favorite songs. This is the defining characteristic of popular music: it finds acceptance with the public and produces profits for songwriters, performers, and publishers. "Minstrelsy was a commercial venture created for a mass market at a time when the United States lacked a definable national culture" (Mahar 1999, 9). The rebellious, anti-social nature of many of minstrelsy's lyrics appealed to the majority of the public. This existed by popular demand. Ticket sales to minstrel shows and sheet music sales were the gauge for the songwriters' lyrical subjects.

Postbellum minstrelsy reflected the change in attitude that accompanied the abolition of slavery and the failure of reconstruction. The themes of the nation's popular music became more racist and expressed violence, hatred, and degrading images that were generally unknown before the Civil War. The characters were no longer slaves, and a sympathetic tone toward blacks was almost gone. Real-life Negroes were no longer non-entities, but competitors with whites, especially for employment. Even Foster, had he lived to write more of his brilliant songs, could not have stopped this degradation of minstrelsy. Despite this, the roots of modern American popular music—rock and roll, country, blues, hip-hop, rap, and jazz—extend deep into musical and cultural history, draw from the best of the antebellum blackface minstrels.

> Minstrelsy may well have been the "national art of its moment," but its impact on the future of American popular music now appears to have been quite significant. Minstrelsy appropriated elements of black culture with varying degrees of accuracy and with an overall purpose of creating a commercially popular product. It provided an early demonstration that Americans were committed to topical entertainment, were sentimental in their perceptions of much deeper emotional issues, misogynistic in their views of gender equality, and resistant to the complex social problems in an environment devoted to play and diversion. . . . Blackface minstrelsy was one of the paradigms for the whole enterprise recognized now as the popular culture industry (Mahar 1999, 353).

After his death, Foster's songs were still popular, but not on the earlier level. However, what his music lacked in immediate popularity it made up in longevity. No other songwriter of the nineteenth century produced songs that are as well known as Foster's. His songs began in the domain of pop culture yet now play continually in the background of the national experience and top the playlist of the American soundtrack.

THE STORY & SPIRIT OF THE ANTEBELLUM BANJO

In 1829, J. L. Frederick of Philadelphia published a popular song called "The Coal Black Rose" that begins with these lines: "Lubly Rosa' Sambo cum / don't you hear de Banjo tum, tum, tum." Thereafter, references to the banjo in popular music were legion. Images of the instrument decorated scores of sheet music covers and it was used in all the minstrel bands that proliferated in every corner of America. However, no banjo is better known than the one that traveled on a slave's knee from Alabama to New Orleans in Stephen Foster's song, "Oh! Susanna." This was the first of many songs Mr. Foster wrote for the minstrel stage that enshrine the antebellum banjo in melody and verse. A recent museum exhibition titled "The Birth Of The Banjo" illuminated that instrument. Its catalog says this:

> The banjo emerged when white Americans first focused on, and attempted to emulate, the music and dance of African Americans. Like Elvis Presley and the Rolling Stones a century later, the first white banjo performers claimed to imitate—and certainly exploited for financial gain—the indigenous Southern rural music of black America. The grotesqueness and mockery with which blackface minstrels "delineated" what they claimed to be accurate renditions of black music and dance still offends, and questions about the degree of authenticity of their renditions continue to occupy scholars. What is incontestable is that this explosively popular music—our country's first mass entertainment—brought the banjo, the only truly American and African-American musical instrument, into the minds and hearts of the American public (Szego 2003, 37).

The instrument we now know as the banjo developed from an African prototype. Its early varieties were often made from a large gourd. A slice was cut off the gourd and that opening was covered with a thin piece of animal skin, similar to a drumhead. This modified gourd was fitted with a neck, and strung with three or four strings. One of these was often a short string plucked only with the thumb. This thumb string, which is now sometimes called the chanterelle, was of either African or African-American origin (Linn 1994, 1).

By the late 1840s, frame-style banjos came into vogue. These had a wooden hoop frame with an open back, animal skin head, five strings, and fretless neck. Its dimensions were large in comparison to a modern banjo. A twelve- to fourteen-inch diameter frame three to four inches deep complemented a very long neck (Gura 1999, 5). The strings were typically made from animal gut, specifically the intestines of ruminant animals. The larger diameter fourth string was often made from copper or silver wound silk fiber. The head could have been made from the skin of any animal, but that of a thin-skinned animal such as a sheep, goat, or calf was preferable. This was made taut by means of a tensioning system consisting of a metal hoop and six or more threaded metal hooks, nuts, and brackets. This allowed adjustment to compensate for the expansion or contraction of the skin due to changes in humidity. The head on gourd banjos and early frame instruments was affixed by means of tacks. This method still existed in the mid-nineteenth century but was not as common as metal tensioning systems since the only way to tighten a tackhead banjo's head was by application of heat. Humidity also effected the tension of the instrument's gut strings.

"The great classical banjoist Albert Baur . . . recalled that in the antebellum period stage performers often had to warm up 'the old tack head banjo' before they could go on stage, sometimes utilizing 'a gaslight or flame from a burning newspaper' for the task" (Ibid., 49).

Various types of wood were utilized for the hoop, neck, dowel, pegs, nut, and tailpiece of these banjos. Following contemporary trends, veneer and false grain finished woods were popular. Friction tuning pegs, similar to those used with violins, adjusted the string tension. By the time of the Civil War (1861), some banjos used machine tuners like those on guitars. After the war, the banjo evolved even further from its African beginnings. For example, the number of tension hooks increased, raised frets became popular, and a guitar-style playing method was codified.

The songs of the big-city minstrel stage was not the music of the slaves but the use of the banjo lent authenticity. The white banjoists' playing style was genuine, however, because they used the slave musicians' method of banjo playing. The earliest white banjoists learned this directly from the black players. It has been preserved to this day in the surviving antebellum banjo instruction books. Latter-day, modified versions of this style are called clawhammer and frailing.

Late in the antebellum era, the minstrels' playing method began to be called banjo style to differentiate it from an emerging technique that was derived from guitar playing. This is mentioned in Tom Briggs' 1855 banjo instructor: "A good imitation of the Banjo can be made on the Guitar, by removing the Sixth String, and putting the First String in its place, and then playing in the Banjo Style." The strings were "struck" in banjo style, whereas in the guitar style the strings were "snapped" (Briggs 1855, 30–31). Today, the minstrels' method of banjo playing is called stroke style.

The antebellum frame banjos with which Stephen Foster was familiar, had a high action and widely spaced strings. These features, coupled with a long scale and gut strings, worked well with minstrel music's melodic style and probably contributed to its relatively slow tempos. "The minstrel banjo was at the heart of the sound of the minstrel ensemble, and it did not sound like a modern banjo. Surviving banjos from the period have a mellower, fuller, more resonant sound" (Bean 1996, 142). Therefore, if modern musicians wish to play the tunes in this book in the way of the blackface minstrels for whom Foster composed them, they should use a reproduction antebellum banjo and the playing technique explained in the early instruction manuals. However, a modern open back banjo strung with nylon may be substituted. The use of a tall, wide bridge will aid in duplicating the correct right hand technique on a modern banjo. However, such an instrument will not correctly reproduce the antebellum sound.

Evidence of how the minstrel performers tuned their banjos is found in the early banjo instruction books. We think that Stephen Foster intended his music to be played with the banjo tuned in the key of G, that is, d G D F# A. Proof of this is found in the sketch of a banjo he made on a sheet of used staff paper (see page 53). In this sketch Foster notes the tuning of each string. This tuning is described in Elias Howe, Jr.'s *The Complete Preceptor for the Banjo* (1850) and in Thomas F. Briggs' *Briggs' Banjo Instructor* (1855). Howe's primary tuning is in the key of F – c F C E G while the G tuning is an alternate. Briggs lists both G tuning and D tuning (d A D F# A). As the antebellum period ended, the popularity of other tunings arose (Winans 1994, 11).

Just as electric guitar takes the lead in rock bands, the banjo was the principle instrument in blackface minstrel bands, whereas fiddle was secondary. The melody was played coincident with the lead vocal. "There were no chords in the ensemble because the banjoist played only a melody; this is evident from banjo methods of the [eighteen] fifties which also describe an older practice" (Nathan 1962, 127).

In his *Banjo Instructor* the famous banjoist Thomas F. Briggs explains early banjo technique. He describes the banjo rim resting on the right thigh while the right forearm rests on the top of the rim. The right wrist is located over the bridge and the hand is above the strings. The neck of the banjo just below the nut rests between the thumb and first finger of the left hand. The fingers of the left hand are separated and prepared to stop the strings. The thumb of the right hand rests on the fifth string. The right hand fingers are held closely together with the first finger slightly farther away from the palm than the other fingers. The fingers are stiff while the wrist is limber.

> In playing, the thumb and first finger only of the right hand are used; the 5th string is touched by the thumb only, this string is always played *open*, the other strings are touched by the thumb and the first finger, the thumb and finger should meet the strings obliquely, so as to cause them to vibrate across the finger-board. The strings are touched by the ball of the thumb, and the nail of the 1st finger. The first finger should strike the strings with the *back of the nail* and then slide to. When using the thumb, the first finger nail should rest against the 1st string; when using the first finger, the thumb should rest on the 5th string; when the first finger strikes any one of the strings, other than the 1st string, the finger should slide to, and rest on the next string to the one struck; when the 1st string is struck, the finger should slide to, and rest on the top of the instrument (Briggs 1855, 8).

This is a good description of the mechanics of antebellum banjo playing, but it goes much further than this. The wonder of the minstrel banjo and the music it makes is in its spirit and ability to transport the listener more than one and a half centuries into the past, to a place that, though still America, was another world. With the left hand, one plays a European melody, with the right, the exciting broken rhythms of Africa. The voice sings words that describe people and places that may be imagined or exaggerated but are somehow very real. All this combines to describe that former world while mysteriously illuminating the present.

I LIKE DAT GOOD OLD SONG
NOTES ON
THE ARRANGEMENTS

Stephen Foster wrote his *Plantation* and *Ethiopian Melodies* to be performed by the wildly popular blackface minstrel troupes of his day. Yet, he also had his eye on another market as well: The piano players of middle class parlors whose musical appetites for sheet music were voracious. For example, in 1852, wholesale book dealer W. M. Cunningham of Mount Vernon, Ohio advertised 5000 pieces of sheet music (Sacks 1993, 229n87). Many of these were certainly titles by Stephen C. Foster published in arrangements for piano. The sale of this sheet music was the songwriter's bread and butter. For that reason Stephen Foster's minstrel tunes were not published as sheet music in arrangements for banjo during his lifetime. Though he intended that they be performed on this instrument, there was no market for banjo sheet music. The mid-nineteenth century American public would have to wait until after the Civil War for wide-scale marketing of the banjo, along with the necessary sheet music. In view of this, we believe that this book is the first publication of Foster's plantation and Ethiopian melodies arranged for minstrel-style banjo.

These arrangements draw on the playing style described in *Brigg's Banjo Instructor,* published in 1855.[1] By learning these songs, a musician will master the elementary techniques used by early banjoists, including those acclaimed on the minstrel stage. However, Mr. Foster not only devised wonderful tunes, he wrote lyrics to match. So, we do not intend that these arrangements stand alone, but that the lyrics be sung along with the tunes. The structure of these tunes and arrangements are, therefore, not as complex as some of the music in the early banjo instructors. They are not meant to display exceptional banjo virtuosity, but to combine with exceptional lyrics to delight the listener and please the performer.

These banjo arrangements naturally follow Mr. Foster's tunes. However, infrequently certain embellishments diverge from the melody. In such cases, we recommend that the user refer to the original sheet music to fill in the melody. This is easily found in the two volumes of *The Music of Stephen Foster.*[2] These rich, comprehensive resources are readily available at public libraries.

Regarding tempo: Note that several of the songs in this book are marked *Moderato,* meaning, "at a moderate pace." Such a pace is between 90 and 115 beats per minute (bpm). Mr. Foster's tempo instruction for "Oh! Lemuel!" is *Not too fast.* This may also indicate a moderate pace. "Away Down Souf," on the other hand, comes with the instruction, *Not too slow,* while "The Glendy Burk" moves along *Moderately fast.* The songwriter left us an interesting detail about tempo with "Don't Bet Your Money On De Shanghai," noting *Moderato con spirito.* Of the more melancholy songs, "My Old Kentucky Home, Good Night!" is marked *Poco Adagio,* which literally means "a little slow tempo." Adagio is commonly counted at 66 to 76 bpm. Per-

---

1 Reprints of this and other early banjo instruction manuals can be purchased from Tuckahoe Music, PO Box 146, Bremo Bluff, VA 23022; 804-842-3573 or Centerstream Publishing LLC, P.O. Box 17878, Anaheim, CA 92817.

2 Saunders, Steven and Deane L. Root. *The Music of Stephen C. Foster, Volumes 1 and 2.* Washington: Smithsonian Institution Press, 1990.

All Banjo music is *written* in the keys of G and D, therefore, when the performer wishes to play in any other keys, he has but to change the *pitch* of the strings, and then play in the key of G or D, producing the *sounds* of whatever key he tuned to. In this manner while it would seem to the performer that he was playing in the key of G, or D, the tones he would produce might be in the key of A♭, or any other remote key he might tune to. It will thus be seen that the Banjo can be played in *any* key.

THE BANJO.

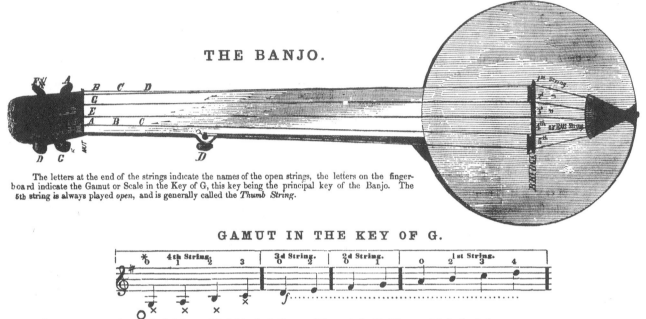

The letters at the end of the strings indicate the names of the open strings, the letters on the finger-board indicate the Gamut or Scale in the Key of G, this key being the principal key of the Banjo. The 5th string is always played *open*, and is generally called the *Thumb String*.

GAMUT IN THE KEY OF G.

O Indicates an open string; 1, the first finger of the *left* hand; 2, the second finger ; 3, the third finger, and 4, the fourth finger.
O× Indicates the thumb of the *right* hand, and F, the first finger.

Illustration from *Brigg's Banjo Instructor of 1855* that shows the suggested tuning of the instrument preferred by Thomas Briggs, a popular antebellum banjoist. *Briggs 1855, 9.*

haps the word *poco* is a hint that we should play the song on the slow end of that range. Foster's note on "Massa's In De Cold Ground" is *Poco Lento* "a little very slow" (Lento: 40–60 bpm). However, while the wanderer in "Old Folks At Home" is sadly roaming up and down the whole creation, he must be traveling at a good clip because Foster asks us to play the song *Moderato*—the same tempo as "Ring De Banjo!"

When considering these tempo notations, we must keep in mind that the original sheet music editions of these songs were arranged for piano. Not only so, it is likely that the original performers of these songs, the antebellum blackface minstrels, took liberties with tempo to serve the purposes of their performances.

OH! SUSANNA
A SONG LIKE NO OTHER

Stephen Foster was a twenty-one-year-old bookkeeper at his brother's firm in Cincinnati when he wrote "Oh! Susanna." He circulated the manuscript to many people, and a copy found its way to Cincinnati music publisher W. C. Peters who sent Foster a fee for the song. "Imagine my delight in receiving one hundred dollars in cash," Foster told a friend. "Oh! Susanna" was published in early 1848 and took the country by storm. However, foreshadowing the young songwriter's difficult career, W. C. Peters eventually made over $10,000 from the song, while Foster had to settle for his hundred dollars (Austin 1975, 11). Not only so, he had to struggle to be recognized as the song's author. However, because it so quickly became America's best-known song, the young man found confidence to take up songwriting full time.

Because "Oh! Susanna" is so very different than any previous minstrel tune, and was such a phenomenal success, the date of its premier performance—September 11, 1847—is considered the day American popular music was born. The fact that its popularity propelled Stephen Foster into full-time, professional songwriting, strengthens this idea. No one in America had ever before taken the step that established the preeminence of the songwriter over the performer of pop music as the pattern in the music industry for the next 100 years.

Rhythmically, the tune is a polka, though somewhat slower than the European dance that had become popular with young Americans at the time. Foster combined this new sound with both serious and comic lyrics that reflect the America of the late 1840s. He decked the song with the typical trappings of minstrelsy—lyrics in dialect, a banjo-playing male slave protagonist, separation of loved ones, a southern setting, nonsensical lyrics, death, the river—and the result is a song like no other.

The lyrics entwine two experiences common to Foster's day—the loss of a loved one and a rapidly changing world. A banjo-playing slave has been separated from his lover—Susanna. The dream of the song's third verse shows that the man's search for her only takes place in his dreams, since slaves could not take interstate journeys for any reason except in service to their masters. This theme of separation among slaves found in "Oh! Susanna" appears time and again in Foster's songs.[1]

When this song is sung today, its second verse is usually left out or, if it is sung, the lyrics are altered. However, without its second verse, "Oh! Susanna" loses its link to events of the day. This verse refers to the telegraph, electricity, and steam powered boats and trains; important elements of the Industrial Revolution that was beginning to dominate the lives of mid-nineteenth century Americans. These new inventions spelled doom for the institution of slavery and the labor-intensive businesses and plantations it served. Hence, this lyric: "De lectrick current magnified and killed five hundred Nigga." On its face, this sentence might be humorous to an audience at a nineteenth-century minstrel show. But, it does not literally refer to the violent demise of five hundred slaves; it refers to the advent of technologies that caused the death of American enterprises that were reliant on mass

---

1 See "Angelina Baker," "Ring De Banjo," De Glendy Burk," "Old Folks At Home," "My Old Kentucky Home, Good Night!," "Massa's In De Cold Ground," "Hard Times Come Again No More" etc.

The cover page to the December 30, 1848, Peters edition of "Susanna (Oh! Susanna)."
It was not the first edition of the song but it represents the way Foster intended
it to be played. It was prepared directly from the original autograph.

labor. This lyric means "that agrarian life and the plantation economy are threatened by progress, that slaves and their owners alike are in danger of becoming road kill on the macadam of a rapidly industrializing America" (Emerson 1998, 134). Some may say that Foster did not understand this at the time, even though he intu-itively expressed it in his art. But our study of the antebellum era indicates that Americans were acutely aware of the drastic transformation occurring in their world. They understood that Foster's lyrics were not mere nonsensical humor, but an entertainingly accurate description of their changing world.

The first page of "Susanna (Oh! Susanna)" from the Peters edition.

The second and third pages from the Peters edition of "Susanna (Oh! Susanna)."

Susanna [Oh! Susanna]
S. C. Foster

Arranged for minstrel banjo by Daniel Partner
from "Songs Of The Sable Harmonists"
Cincinati: Peters, Field & Co., 1848

Tuning: d, A, D, F#, A

AWAY DOWN SOUF
THE SECOND-PRIZE WINNER

If, in 1847, there could have been a B-side to "Oh! Susanna," "Away Down Souf" fit the bill. That year, Morrison Foster encouraged his younger brother to write a song to enter into a local competition. A minstrel group performing at the Eagle Ice Cream Saloon in Pittsburgh sang each song that was entered. The notice of the contest informed interested parties:

> A PRIZE OF A SILVER CUP
> will be awarded to the author of such original words of an Ethiopian Melody or Extravaganzas—to be set to music by the present Troupe, as shall be decided by the spontaneous voice of the audience at the TRIAL CONCERT, MONDAY EVENING, Sept. 6. (Morneweck 1944, 312).

The songwriter was to enter a song with both lyrics and music. The term *set to music*, means that the musicians would play that song. Therefore, Foster wrote "Away Down Souf," and his brother entered it into the contest for him. The song finished a close second. The following week, September 11, the same minstrel group held a concert that featured "Away Down Souf" along with another new song by Stephen Foster—"Oh! Susanna."

"Away Down Souf" was published at the end of 1848, but was not nearly as successful as "Oh! Susanna." Officially, however, it was Foster's first minstrel song. The lyrics describe plantation life as Northern audiences may have envisioned it. The horse races and various card games of the first verse give the impression that there is nothing but fun, away down south. The second verse demonstrates Mr. Foster's agility with words. It

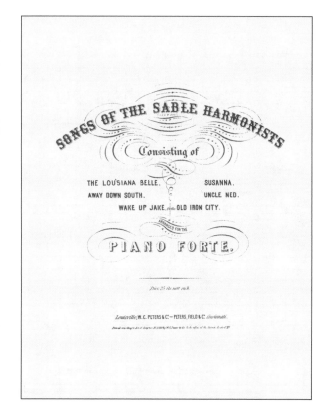

burlesques the size of a black woman's mouth with an image of cutting-edge technology—a railroad car. In the third verse, the audience is pleased to learn that this slave woman lives in a two-story house, however improbable that may have been. All the while, the song's chorus describes America's Southland as verdant with growth, extending all the way to Cuba where the slaves dance a dance that has never been seen before or since—the polka-juba.

Away Down Souf
S. C. Foster

Arranged for minstrel banjo by Daniel Partner
from "Songs Of The Sable Harmonists"
Cincinnati: Peters, Field & Co., 1848

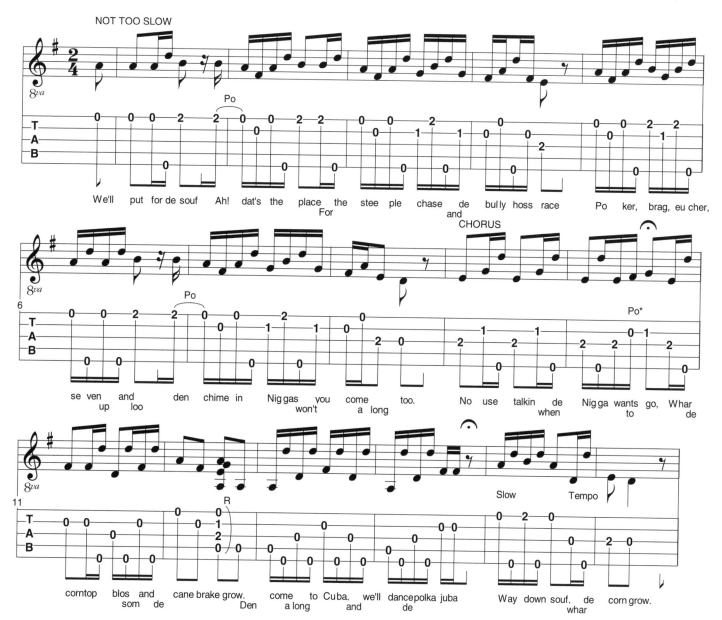

* Pull-off from first position.
Tuning: d, A, D, F#, A

MY BRUDDER GUM
TWO CENTS A COPY

In 1849, Stephen Foster entered into a business relationship with the New York publisher Firth, Pond, and Company, submitting "My Brudder Gum," "Nelly Was A Lady," and "Dolcy Jones" for publication. America's first professional songwriter was on his way to prominence. Here is the agreement he made:

S. C. Foster, Esq.

Dear Sir:

Your favor of 8th inst. is received and we hasten to reply. We will accept the proposition therein made, viz. to allow you two cents upon every copy of your future publications issued by our house, after the expenses of publication are paid, of course it is always our interest to push them as widely as possible. From your acquaintance with the proprietors or managers of the different bands of "minstrels," & from your known reputation, you can undoubtedly arrange with them to sing them.... It is also advisable to compose only such pieces as likely both in the sentiment & melody to take the public taste....

We remain in the hope of hearing from you soon.

Very truly yours,

FIRTH, POND & CO. (Morneweck 1944 I, 354)

"My Brudder Gum" has all the elements that Firth, Pond, and Company was looking for in a marketable song. It uses a supposed Negro dialect and includes fanciful descriptions of plantation life. Its references to the banjo and a catchy melody were just what the public wanted. The song didn't have the popularity of "Oh! Susanna" but at least the songwriter was making money with each piece of sheet music sold. Plus, the top minstrel bands played Foster's songs, which helped sell his sheet music. Here we see the beginning of the popular music industry as we know it today.

As in many songs of the era, different spellings of the same word are found on the sheet music

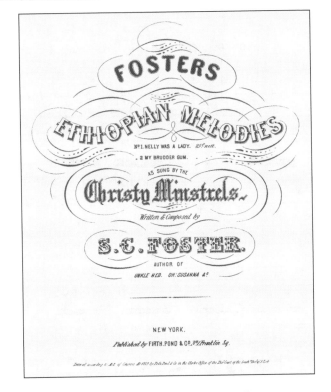

copy. Both "Brodder" and "Brudder" appear on the first edition. Foster may have written it this way; either, by mistake or with a purpose unknown to us.

The refrain of this song mentions "de yaller galls," which translated from the minstrel's dialect is *the yellow girls*. The word *yellow* was used in the nineteenth century to describe mulattos or persons of both white and black parentage. Because their skin was lighter in color, literature and song depicted such women as highly desirable to male slaves. This idea is clearly seen in a minstrel song that Firth, Pond, and Company published in 1858 named "The Yellow Rose of Texas." This song's chorus declares, "She's the sweetest rose of color this darkey ever knew." Mitch Miller popularized "The Yellow Rose of Texas in 1955 in a recording released through Columbia Records, in which this line is changed to, "She's the sweetest little rosebud that Texas ever knew. "

My Brodder Gum
S. C. Foster

Arranged for Minstrel Banjo by Daniel Partner
from "Foster's Ethiopian Melodies No. 2"
New York : Firth, Pond & Co., No. 1 Franklin Sq., 1849

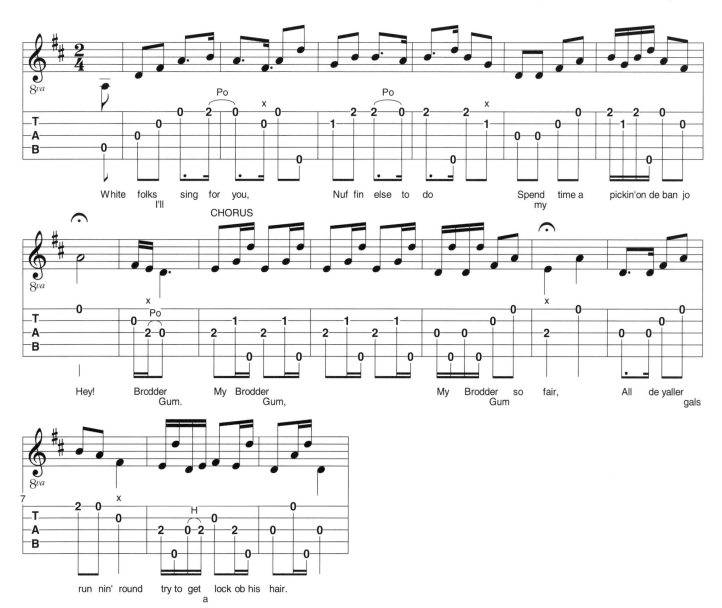

A small x above the tablature indicates a thumb stroke.
Tuning: d, A, D, F#, A

OH! LEMUEL!
THE CELEBRATORY SLAVE

Stephen Foster wrote "Oh! Lemuel!" in early 1850. Some of his most popular minstrel songs—"De Camptown Races," "Nelly Bly," "Angelina Baker," and "Way Down In Ca-i-ro"— all appeared in this, one of the best years of his career. Minstrelsy continued to be all the rage in America, not in small part because Foster knew what made a minstrel song popular.

The title "Oh! Lemuel!" echoes the immensely successful "Oh! Susanna." However, unlike "Oh! Susanna," a song of separation, "Oh! Lemuel!" tells of celebration. Perhaps this is why Foster added the extra exclamation point at the end of the title. The song has all the classic elements of a popular minstrel hit. Set on a cotton plantation, it mentions a popular minstrel figure, Nelly Bly, and like many songs in this genre, "Oh! Lemuel!" points out stereotypical black physical characteristics:

> But if you want to dance,
> Just dance outside de door;
> Becayse your feet so berry large
> Dey'll cover all de floor.

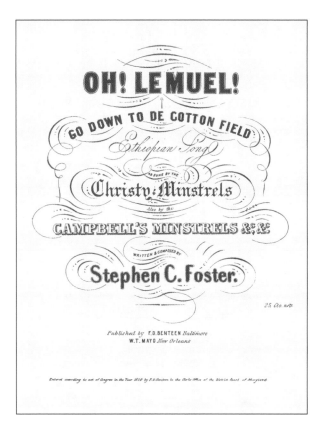

Of course the banjo is here, together with the fiddle and the jawbone, the minstrel's Negro dialect and idealized descriptions of the life of a slave:

> Oh! Lem! Lem! Lem! Lemuel I say!
> Go down to de cotton field and bring de boys away.

This song artfully propagates the idea that plantation life was joyful. The boys in the above lyric took the rest of the day off because they were all going to the ball that night with Nelly Bly, Julianna Snow, and Cane Break Kitty, who "likes de boys." A life of hard work was the truth of plantation life for a slave with very little time of joy.

By this time, Mr. Foster's songs had become so popular that many unauthorized versions were appearing. "Oh! Lemuel!" was often duplicated. "In *Godey's Lady's Book* for August 1850, Professor Grobe is commended for "the taste and skill with which he has prepared variations on 'Oh! Lemuel!' that favorite melody" (Morneweck II 1944, 382).

With few exceptions, all the characters in minstrel songs are slaves like Lemuel. Names for slaves—names like Pompey, Romulus, and Dinah—were commonly chosen from the Bible or Greek and Roman history and mythology. The happy character in this song drew his name from the last chapter of Proverbs, which is devoted to "the words of King Lemuel" (31:1).

Oh! Lemuel! (Go Down To De Cotton Field)
Stephen. C. Foster

Arranged for minstrel banjo by Daniel Partner
from "Oh! Lemuel! Go Down To De Cotton Field"
Baltimore: F. D. Benteen, 1850

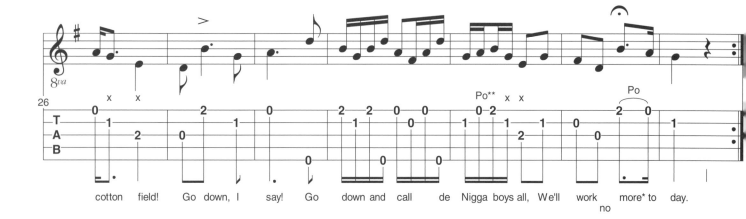

cotton field! Go down, I say! Go down and call de Nigga boys all, We'll work no more* to day.

A small x above the tablature indicates a thumb stroke.
* The pause over the word "more" is to be used only in the repetition of the chorus.
** Pull-off from the second position.
Tuning: d, A, D, F#, A

Half plate ferrotype of reproduction antebellum banjo, tambourine, and bones.
By William Dunniway, 2007.

Cover of the first complete method published for the banjo.
The "Briggs' Banjo Instructor" (1855) by Thomas F. Briggs.

NELLY BLY
A DULCEM MELODY

"Nelly Bly" was a huge hit, and financially rewarding for its composer, hence, 1850 started right for Stephen Foster. Written in dialect, it describes a slave couple's love and domestic tranquility. The old banjo is again referenced in an attempt to confirm that minstrelsy authentically represented the life of plantation slaves. We know today the minstrel's performances were not a true representation of this, but they worked for the audiences of that day, transporting them to a far away, exotic locale.

"Oh! Susanna" was so popular that its melody was used in combination with countless other lyrics. The same was true for "Nelly Bly." For example, in 1860, its tune was used for a presidential campaign song that appeared, apparently without Foster's approval, in the "Republican Songster":

> Hi! Lincoln, Ho! Lincoln! An honest man for me:
> I'll sing for you—I'll shout for you, the People's nominee.

Minstrel songs often include references to other minstrel songs. For example, this song begins with Nelly Bly sweeping her kitchen in preparation for a song. The audiences would recognize this as a reference to "Clare De Kitchen," a popular song of the 1830s performed by Thomas "Daddy" Rice and George Washington Dixon, early solo blackface performers. Here is its first verse:

> In old Kentuck in de arternoon,
> We sweep de floor wid a bran new broom,
> And arter that we form a ring,
> And dis de song dat we do sing.[1]

This sweeping may have its source in the ritualistic folk-theater of the medieval mummers in the British Isles. These groups, including characters in blackface, often performed in the kitchens of private homes that were changed from their common use into the place for the mystery of the mummers' resurrection drama by a ceremonial sweeping of the floor (Cockrell 1997, 47–50).

The quality and effect of Foster's minstrel songs were far above those of his contemporaries because he was so accomplished at "utilizing resonant poetic images with memorable melody" (Saunders 1990, xxxviii), and because his "musical gestures cut across the accepted stylistic boundaries" (Ibid., xxvi). Nelly Bly is a perfect example of the increase in the caliber of antebellum pop music that occurred by the hand of this talented man. The banjoist of "Nelly Bly" promises to sing and play a dulcem melody for his ladylove. Indeed, this song's "peculiar sweetness only carries to an extreme a quality that distinguishes most of Foster's tunes from those of his rivals in the minstrel tradition" (Austin 1975, 81).

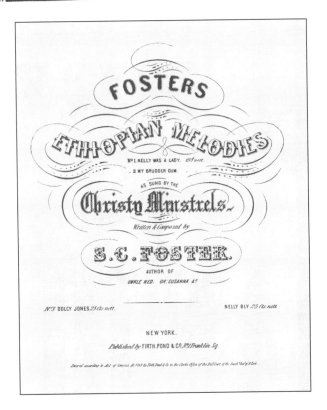

Nelly Bly
S. C. Foster

Arranged for minstrel banjo by Daniel Partner
from "Fosters Ethiopian Melodies. No. 4"
New York: Firth, Pond & Co., 1 Franklin Square, 1850

Tuning: d, A, D, F#, A

GWINE TO RUN ALL NIGHT
OR
DE CAMPTOWN RACES
THE ENCHANTMENT OF DOO-DAH

In his correspondence, Stephen Foster referred to the song we now know as "De Camptown Races" as "Gwine To Run All Night," whereas early sheet music used both titles in this way: "Gwine To Run All Night or De Camptown Races." There are various definitions of a camptown. In the African country of Lesotho a camptown is a district capitol. A town in Pennsylvania, not far where Foster lived for awhile, is named Camptown. And a camptown may simply be a temporary town.

The two most familiar songs of the 19th century to modern Americans have to be "Oh! Susanna" and "Gwine To Run All Night." While "Oh! Susanna's" theme is one of separation, "Gwine To Run All Night" is the complete opposite. The comical song describes a farcical day at the horse races.

Foster added a special feature to his minstrel elements in this song. He wrote the words "Doo-dah" to be sung by the chorus preceded by the solo lyrics in imitation of the field slaves call and singing style of music. Doo-dah is one of the most memorable words in American popular music. Today we pronounce this word *dōōdäh*, with the a in "dah" like that in "father." However, we believe that singers in Foster's day pronounced it *dōōdæ*. That is, the a in "dah" sounded like that in "hat". There are two reasons for our proposing this pronunciation: We're told, "The second syllable of the little refrain, 'Doo-

dah!' is pronounced dah as in dandy, not daw as in dark. At least, that is the way Morrison [Foster] sang it" (Morneweck I 1944, 377). Also, it is consistent with the black dialect in which the song is written to pronounce "dah" with the short a. Be that as it may, the fact that Foster could incorporate such a word in a hit song epitomizes his astonishing gift.

Gwine To Run All Night or De Camptown Races

Stephen C. Foster

Arranged for minstrel banjo by Daniel Partner
from "Foster's Plantation Melodies No. 3"
Baltimore: F.D. Benteen, 1850

Tuning: d, A, D, F#, A

ANGELINA BAKER
THE SOLD-AWAY SLAVE

Both "Oh! Susanna" and "Angelina Baker" are songs of separation. However, the male slave in "Oh! Susanna" travels in search of his love, while in this song, published in 1850, the man is left behind, lamenting his loss. Many minstrel songs stereotypically depict slavery according to certain popular concepts, yet they rarely mention why slave families were separated. Other than death, the most common cause of separation was by sale. Whereas "Oh! Susanna" depicts this with sad lyrics and a cheerful polka melody, Angelina Baker's comparatively melancholy melody matches its sad lyrics.

The well-known folk song, "Angeline the Baker" is derived from "Angelina Baker," though it is only a shadow of Foster's song. Parts of the original melody are still present while its lyrics are entirely different. Most significantly, Angelina is no longer a sold-away slave. This is a shame, since the theme is such an important one in many of Foster's songs. "Angelina Baker" directly addresses the debate over the future of slavery that became unavoidable in 1850: Angelina "used to run old Massa round to ax him for to free dem."

It is ironic that "Angelina Baker" survives even in a modified form when few of Fosters more popular songs do so. For example, very few people today know of "Oh! Lemuel" even though it outsold "Angelina Baker" three to one while Foster was living (Howard 1962, 271).

After Angelina Baker is sold away, the singer is left to "weep a tear and beat on de old jawbone." The jawbone was a percussion instrument sometimes employed by blackface minstrel groups. Other contemporaneous songs mention it as well, most notably "De Ole Jawbone."[1] When the complete jawbone of a large farm animal is beat

against the heel of the hand, its teeth, which rest loose but secure in their settings, shake together and emit a primordial clatter. The use of the jawbone enhanced the minstrels' fanciful portrayal of southern slaves. Whether or not slaves actually used the jawbone as a musical instrument was of little concern to the blackface minstrels. What mattered was that the audience believed they did. (Bean 1996, 143).

---

1 De Ole Jaw Bone. Boston: Henry Prentiss, 33 Court St., 1848.

Angelina Baker
Stephen C. Foster

Arranged for minstrel banjo by Daniel Partner
from "Foster's Plantation Melodies No. 4"
Baltimore: F. D. Benteen, 1850

A small x above the tablature indicates a thumb stroke.
Tuning: d, A, D, F#, A

WAY DOWN IN CA·I·RO
DEATH UP NORTH

A songwriting spree in early 1850 produced eleven of Mr. Foster's published songs. One of these was "Way Down In Ca-i-ro." Cairo, Illinois was a growing town at that time, located at the southernmost tip of Illinois, at the convergence of the Ohio and Mississippi Rivers. Between 1835 and 1840 the town started to boom and by the end of 1840 its population was 2,000. Then it boasted a levee system, dry dock, shipyard, sawmills, iron works, warehouses, and many homes. The southern states shipped millions of pounds of cotton, sugar, wool, and other products to Cairo where the Illinois Central Railroad carried it to Chicago and points beyond.

The town's name, *Cairo,* is correctly pronounced kā-rō, unlike Cairo, Egypt, which is pronounced kī-rō. However, in Foster's song, it is pronounced kā-ī-rō—a mashup of both pronunciations. This is emphasized in the hyphenated title. Perhaps he devised this pronunciation to fit with the so-called Negro dialect used in minstrelsy. More likely: he needed three syllables so his lyrics would scan.

The song repeatedly voices this fear: "'Way down in Ca-i-ro dis nigga's guine to die." The laborers that harvested and transported goods on the Ohio and Mississippi Rivers were mostly slaves. Cairo was a world away from a slave's home and family in the South; not a desirable place to die. We can imagine the man depicted in "The Glendy Burk" in the regions of Cairo, Illinois as he mowed in a hay field dreaming of his return to the sunny old South.

The first verse of this song is an introduction for a stage performance in which the audience is assured, "I only mean to please you all, and den I's guine away." The following three verses contrast the weeping and dying found in the chorus by describing a pleasant life in slavery—a discor-

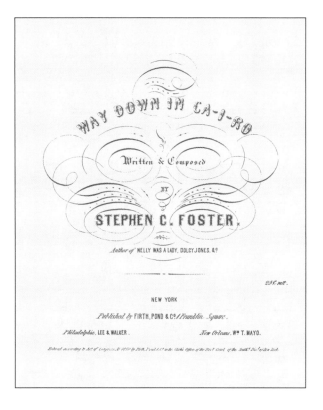

dant thought to the modern mind, but entertaining to many mid-nineteenth Americans. The happy slave sings all day long, and, when there is no food, she sweeps the kitchen clean. The third verse proposes this ridiculous scene: "Massa bought a bran new coat and hung it on the wall, Dis nigga's guine to take dat coat, and wear it to de ball." Did Foster write that the slave was going to wear his master's coat only for the humor of it or to vocalize the secret wish of many slaves—to possess a brand new coat? The final verse boasts of the success of the darkey band that performs this song. It was only a small exaggeration at the time to say, "All the ladies in the land and all the gemmen too" were clamoring for the music that Stephen Foster and his contemporaries were writing for the blackface minstrel stage.

Way Down In Ca-i-ro

Stephen C. Foster

Arranged for minstrel banjo by Daniel Partner
from "Way Down In Ca-i-ro"
New York: Firth, Pond & Co., 1 Franklin Square, 1850

A small x above the tablature indicates a thumb stroke.
Tuning: d, A, D, F#, A

RING, RING DE BANJO!
THE MASTER STORYTELLER

Celebrating the banjo, the king-instrument of the minstrel stage, and enlisting one of minstrelsy's best-known characters, "Ring, Ring De Banjo!" reveals Stephen Foster's great gift of storytelling. It tells of a runaway slave, the death of his master, and separation from his lover, Susanna. As usual, the song's protagonist is a care-free fellow who, though a slave, is at leisure to roam the old plantation in the company of his true love, philosophize, sing songs, and play the banjo, the piano, and even the bones—a rare appearance in song lyrics of the minstrel percussionist's preferred instrument.

As in other minstrel songs of the time Foster has the male slave being set free but then returning "Others left but before long felt compelled to return: 'Shaw! what's de use ob going 'mong strangers in de West?/We'd best stay here, whar we are near, wid old massa an' de rest.'" (Toll 1974, 85).

The fourth verse opens early one summer morning. Suddenly, as he plays a dulcem tune, his "Massa fall a napping, he'll never wake again." As it was on the mind of many slaves this was a popular minstrel element.

A year later, in 1852, Foster wrote an entire song about the death of Ole Massa in "Massa's In De Cold Ground." The Boston music publisher Oliver Ditson published a successful minstrel song in 1846 titled "De Blue Tailed Fly." Written by an unknown author, this song is also about the death of a slave's master without the nostalgic melancholy of Foster's song. Here it describes his death:

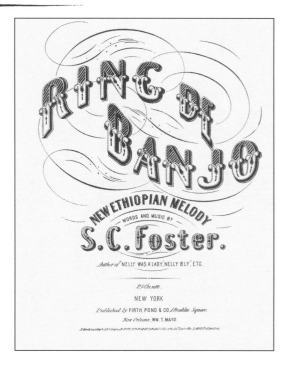

> De poney run, he jump, an pitch,
> An tumble massa in de ditch;
> He died, an de Jury wonder why,
> De verdict was de "blue tail fly."

Despite his earlier promise to go away no more, the slave of "Ring, Ring De Banjo!" declares, "My lub, I'll hab to leabe you," promising that he'll return to redeem her. One problem: He foolishly chooses to flee "while de ribber's running high." That is, at the wrong season of the year—a humorous turn of events when portrayed by a blackface minstrel. At the end of the song, despite his pledge to return for Susanna, it is doubtful he'll ever reach the Promised Land.

In this story, the reader can discern key components that distinguished minstrel songs in the antebellum era. However, these reliable elements did not succeed in lifting this song to the level of popularity of Mr. Foster's earlier compositions (Tasker 1962, 267).

Musically, "Ring, Ring De Banjo!" displays a pleasing syncopation, the broken rhythm of African music that made its crossover into the American mainstream when white musicians learned to play the banjo from enslaved musicians. Fifty years after "Ring, Ring De Banjo!" was published, syncopation flooded pop music during the ragtime craze at the turn of the twentieth century.

Ring, Ring de Banjo!
S. C. Foster

Arranged for minstrel banjo by Daniel Partner
from "Ring De Banjo. New Ethiopian Melody"
New York: Firth, Pond & Co., 1 Franklin Square, 1851

Tuning: d, A, D, F#, A

37

OH! BOYS CARRY ME 'LONG
THE BEGINNING OF MELANCHOLY

In this song, we witness the songwriter making a transition from hardcore minstrel songs, such as "Oh! Lemuel!," to a softer approach to the minstrels' subject matter. It foreshadows the melancholic feeling of Stephen Foster's hit songs of 1851–53. He still used dialect in some of those songs, but "Oh! Boys Carry Me 'Long" is the last song to use the word *nigga*. Here, we witness Mr. Foster's remarkable empathetic capacity as he describes a slave's death after a lifetime of servitude. The voice of that slave puts into words the common belief of those held in chattel bondage that their only way to freedom is through death. So, we hear the old man sing, "Oh! carry me 'long; der's no more trouble for me: I's guine to roam in a happy home where all de niggas am free."

Scholars wonder if the songwriter's more sorrowful minstrel songs were performed seriously or sardonically. In other words, did the entertainers play them for laughs, regardless of the subject matter, or did they aspire to draw out their audiences' sympathy for the songs' characters? Many of Foster's compositions are comical, but others are sad. Certainly, each song was presented differently depending upon the performers' sensibility, and perhaps that of the audience as well. Ken Emerson, Foster's most recent biographer, believes this song was not presented melancholically as the lyrics would have one believe. He writes, "It's hard to imagine the song being performed with a straight face" (Emerson 1998, 178). Foster, however, wrote this to the performer E. P. Christy regarding "Oh! Boys Carry Me 'Long" in a letter dated June 20, 1851: "Remember it should be sung in a pathetic, not

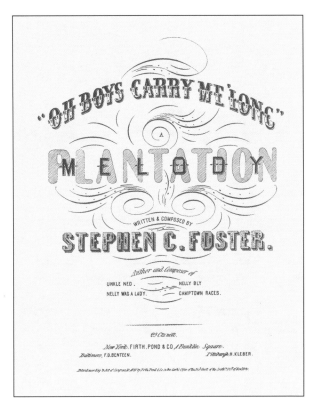

a comic style." Mr. Foster's niece, Evelyn Foster Morneweck, tells us, "Stephen shows that, as a composer, he was very particular about the way his works were presented to the public, and was anxious that the mood that attended the writing of 'Oh! Boys Carry Me 'Long' should be shared by the singer" (Morneweck II 1944, 397).

This song was quite popular and ranks fifth in total sales of the composer's minstrel songs of the 1850s (Howard 1943, 267). Today, it is never performed, except by the authors, and soon, we hope, by some of our readers.

Oh! Boys, Carry Me 'Long
Stephen C. Foster

Arranged for minstrel banjo by Daniel Partner
from "Songs Of The Sable Harmonists"
New York: Firth & Pond, 1 Franklin Square, 1851

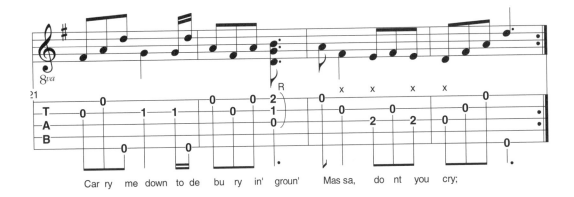

Tuning: A, F#, D, A, d

(*left*) An image of antebellum musicians with banjo and bones. It is possibly a daguerreotype but identified as an ambrotype.

(*above*) An ambrotype of an antebellum banjo player. "JS Little 1857" is on the banjo head. Hand coloring portions of images were common in the time before color photography.

OLD FOLKS AT HOME
A CATCHING, MELODIC ITCH

"Old Folks At Home" is one of the world's most famous songs (Howard 1962, 193). Perhaps this is because it successfully straddles the divide between the parlor and the minstrel stage. Ken Emerson, in his biography of Stephen Foster, observes, "Anybody could sing it, and everybody did. While Christy's Minstrels were belting it out at Mechanics' Hall, the actress Emily Mestayer was singing it at Barnum's nearby museum" (Emerson 1998, 181–182). A contemporary New York newspaper wrote, "The song . . . absolutely the rage everywhere, having no rival unless it was 'Ben Bolt'. Every band, some borrowed from as far as Nyack, was playing 'Old Folks At Home' in the streets of New York (Ibid., 182)."

Foster knew what audiences wanted and, as with so many of his other minstrel songs, he delivered this to them. Emerson relates that "one reviewer called the 'homely tune' a 'catching, melodic itch of the times . . . and nearly everyone scratched, be they Irish or German immigrants feeling homesick for the old country, frontiersmen or forty-niners pining for the folks they had left behind in the East, or African Americans forcibly separated from their birthplaces and families, 'Old Folks At Home' was all things to all people (Ibid.)."

Despite the song's popularity, Foster was unhappy that he'd sold the right to have his name on the published sheet music. Even though he received all the royalties from the song, and soon became known as its true author, it was the name of the leader of Christy's Minstrels, E. P. Christy, that adorned the music during Foster's lifetime. We don't know why Mr. Foster allowed Christy to claim authorship, but this was ill advised since "Old Folks At Home" is one of his finest songs.

Today, "Old Folks At Home" is well known and often performed, and is the official song of the State of Florida. The Swanee River of Foster's song is the Suwannee River, which flows out of the Okeefenokee Swamp in Georgia, through Florida, and into the Gulf of Mexico. The Sunshine State re-titled the song "The Swanee River," though it kept the original lyrics and dialect, and did not excise or change the word *darkies,* as did Kentucky when it appropriated "My Old Kentucky Home."

The subject of the song is a male slave who has either escaped the plantation or is for some reason free to travel. The former may be the case since he doesn't seem to have the freedom to return and visit his folks at home. Instead, he must sadly roam "all up and down the whole creation." Another biographer of Foster puts forward the idea that "Old Folks" is the songwriter's lamentation over the loss of his carefree childhood days—a nearly universal sentiment. "His refrain, with a melody that rises above the rest of the song on the words, 'All de world,' suggests that he and his sympathizers might still be 'sad and dreary' even if the wish [to return home] were fulfilled: the happiness of childhood cannot remain available; the most we can hope for is to die, comforted by a mother" (Austin 1975, 247).

Three of the songs in this book were used extensively in musical stage adaptations of Harriet Beecher Stowe's novel *Uncle Tom's Cabin.* These are, "Old Folks At Home," "Massa's In De Cold Ground," and "My Old Kentucky Home." Each of these was written at the time *Uncle Tom's Cabin* gained its phenomenal popularity, so one cannot help but assume that in writing them, Stephen Foster was influenced by the novel itself and/or its profound effect on American popular thought.

Old Folks At Home

E. P. Christy [Stephen C. Foster]

Arranged for minstrel banjo by Daniel Partner
from "Old Folks at Home. Ethiopian Melody"
New York: Firth, Pond & Co., 1851

MODERATO

Way down on de Swa nee rib ber, Far, far a way,
up

Dere's whar heart turn ing eb ber, Dere's whar old folks stay.
my is de

All up and down whole crea a tion, sad ly I roam,
de

Still long ing for de old plan ta tion, And for de old folks at home.

All de world am sad and drear y Eb' ry where I roam;

Oh! dark eys how my heart grows wea ry, Far from old folks at home.

Ad. lib.

de

Tuning: d, A, D, F#, A

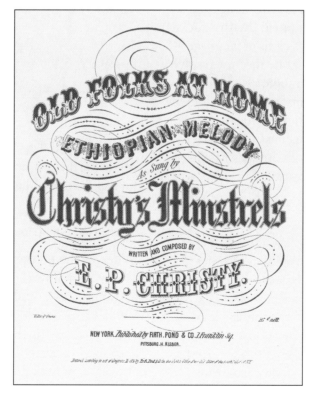

43

MASSA'S IN DE COLD GROUND
AN ENDURING
STEREOTYPE

Stephen Foster published only four songs in 1852. However, the first of these, "Massa's In De Cold Ground" was quite successful. This song was the last minstrel song written in the Negro dialect until "The Glendy Burk" appeared in 1860. Many reasons have been given regarding why Foster temporarily abandoned dialect. We feel that the most reasonable of these is that it was commercially advantageous for him to do so. By this time, Foster was writing with more of an eye to sales than he was earlier in his career, writing both minstrel and parlor songs. While the minstrel songs were the more popular, the wholesomeness of the parlor songs may have been more attractive to him. A biographer says that at this time he was "still struggling to reconcile commercial appeal with social respectability, confronting a crisis of language—of diction and dialect—that he did not resolve until year's end" (Emerson 1998, 185).

Even though Foster temporarily abandoned dialect, he was by no means planning on forsaking the money-making business of minstrelsy. In a letter to the founder of Christy's Minstrels on May 25, 1852, Foster wrote:

E.P. Christy, Esq.
Dear Sir:
As I once intimated to you, I had the intention of omitting my name on my Ethiopian songs, owing to the prejudice against them by some, which might injure my reputation as a writer of another style of music, but I find that by my efforts I have done a great deal to build up a taste for the Ethiopian songs among refined people by making the words suitable to their taste, instead of the trashy and really offensive words which belong to some songs of that order. Therefore, I have concluded to reinstate my name on my songs and to pursue the Ethiopian business without fear or

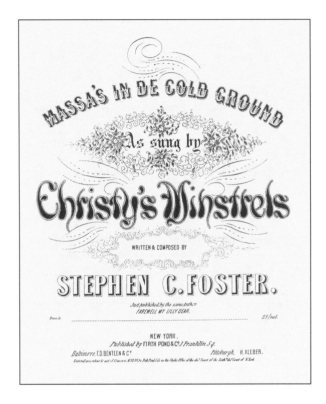

shame, and lend all my energies to making the business live, at the same time that I will wish to establish my name as the best Ethiopian songwriter. . .

Very respectfully yours,
Stephen C. Foster (Howard 1962, 196–197)

Whereas the theme of lamenting the loss of a slave by his fellow slaves as in "Oh! Boys Carry Me 'Long" was popular, Foster reversed this in "Massa's In De Cold Ground." Here, the slaves lament the loss of their beloved master. With meadow, mockingbird, and mounded grave, darkies weeping in the cornfield, an orange tree, sandy shore, and ever-present banjo, the songwriter eloquently painted the stereotypical plantation scene that sold sheet music.

Massa's In De Cold Ground
Stephen C. Foster

Arranged for minstrel banjo by Daniel Partner
from "Massa's in de Cold Ground"
New York: Firth, Pond & Co., 1 Franklin Sq., 1852

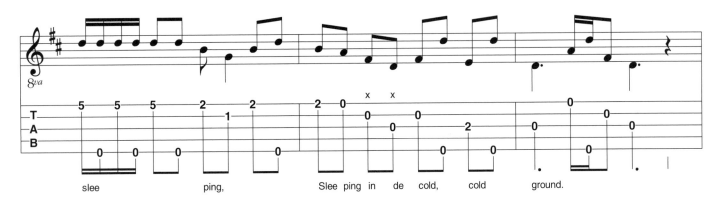

slee ping, Slee ping in de cold, cold ground.

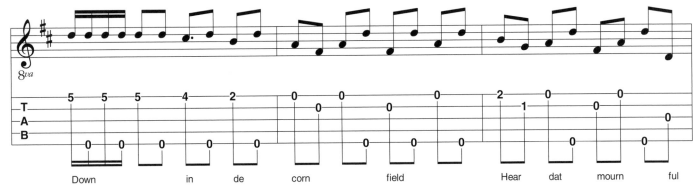

Down in de corn field Hear dat mourn ful

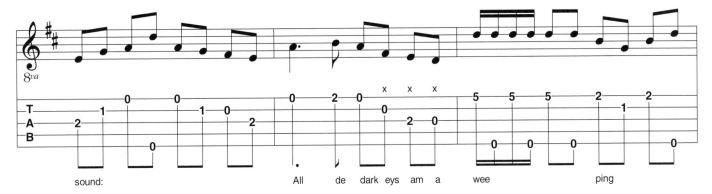

sound: All de dark eys am a wee ping

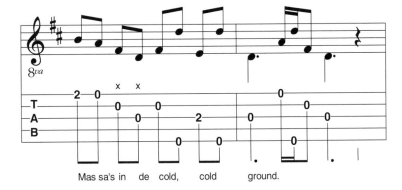

Mas sa's in de cold, cold ground.

A small x above the tablature indicates a thumb stroke.
Tuning: d, A, D, F#, A

MY OLD KENTUCKY HOME, GOOD-NIGHT!
THE INTOLERABLE BURDEN

This hit song of 1853 was Stephen Foster's first minstrel song not written in dialect, and the last to use the word *darkey*. Just as "Old Folks At Home" is the official state song of Florida, "My Old Kentucky Home, Good-Night!" is the official state song of Kentucky. Whereas Florida kept the original lyrics to "Old Folks At Home" and changed its title to "The Swanee River," Kentucky modified the title of Foster's song to "My Old Kentucky Home," and made one change in the lyrics: The word *darkies,* which is used once in the song, has been changed to "people." We feel that if one wishes to keep Foster's intent in his lyrics, yet omit the word *darkies*, the replacement word should be "slaves."

"My Old Kentucky Home, Good-Night!" is typical of "all of Stephen's melancholy Negro songs [which] reveal that he was decidedly fatalistic about the institution of slavery. He seemed to regard it as an intolerable burden under which the black race stumbled helplessly and hopelessly. With a kind master, he pictured them carefree and happy enough, but he seemed to glimpse no freedom ahead for them in this world" (Emerson 1997, 195).

The first verse and chorus of this song are sung, with some shedding of tears, at the running of the Kentucky Derby. Its title is also inscribed on the reverse of the current US state series quarter for Kentucky. We know of no other song title that has been memorialized on US currency. This is the latest big hit for Stephen C. Foster. However, we suggest that, in keeping with the subject of Mr. Foster's song, a slave's cabin and a mule replace the stately house and thoroughbred horse depicted on the coin.

"My Old Kentucky Home, Good Night!" was Foster's response to Harriet Beecher Stowe's novel *Uncle Tom's Cabin; or, Life Among The Lowly,* (1852), which was, except for the Bible, the best selling book of the nineteenth century. Indeed, the first draft of this song was titled "Poor Uncle Tom, Good Night." Even though minstrelsy is denounced in Stowe's book, its huge popularity was an asset to this song's success in part because it was often sung during the stage adaptations of *Uncle Tom's Cabin.*

> By writing a plantation ballad in nearly Standard English, Foster overcame the blackface/parlor ballad, possum fat/flowrets dichotomy that had long bedeviled him. Second, he eliminated the references to Uncle Tom, freeing the song from the novel, its politics, and its period, and thereby evoking nearly timeless and universal emotions about losing one's family, home, and childhood. When "[t]he day goes by like a shadow o'er the heart," it touches almost everyone's (Morneweck II 1944, 409–410).

Mr. Foster's work in the remaining years of the 1850s indicate that the success of "My Old Kentucky Home, Good-Night!" may have influenced him to shift away from writing music for the minstrel stage. After the publication of this song, seven years would pass before the songwriter revisited the music of minstrelsy.

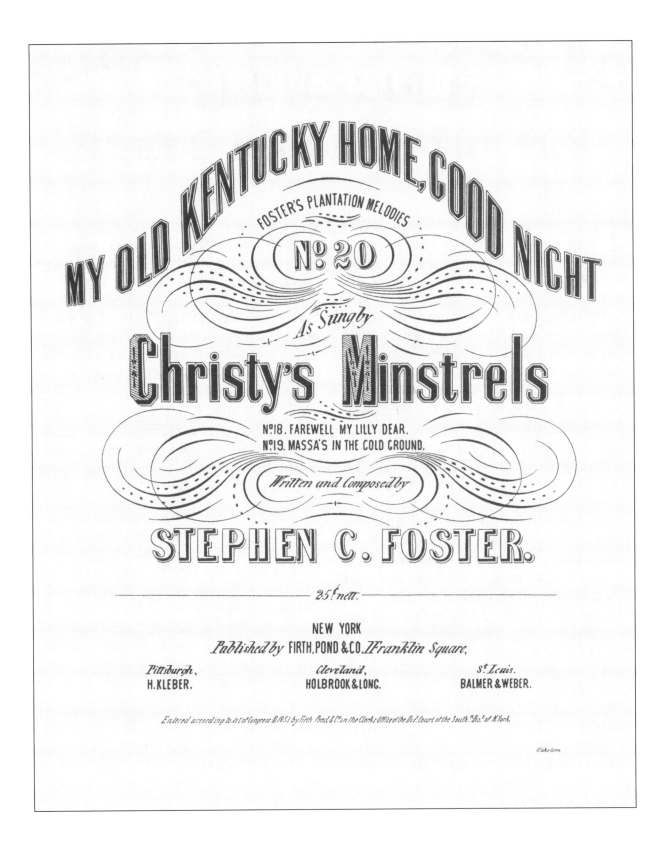

My Old Kentucky Home, Good-Night!
Stephen C Foster

Arranged for minstrel banjo by Daniel Partner
from "Foster's Plantation Melodies. No. 20"
New York: Firth, Pond & Co. 1 Franklin Square, 1853

Tuning: d, A, D, F#, A

THE GLENDY BURK
THE YEARNING
OF A FREEDMAN

Stephen Foster had not written a minstrel song for seven years when he returned to the genre that made him famous. However, fame didn't draw him back to minstrelsy, fortune did. He wrote "The Glendy Burk" (1860) out of financial necessity. He had published numerous parlor songs since "My Old Kentucky Home, Good Night!" appeared in 1853. Notable among these are "Jeanne With The Light Brown Hair" and "Hard Times Come Again No More." Yet, as the number of parlor songs increased, Foster's sales decreased. So, minstrel music was a good bet for the veteran songwriter, since it was as popular as ever. But, by then Foster had been left behind by a new wave of songwriters. Yet, even a veteran like Dan Emmett (1815–1904), one of the original minstrel songwriters and performers, had a hit in 1860 when he published the minstrel song "I Wish I Was In Dixie's Land," the song we now know as "Dixie."

Although the word *the* is used instead of *de* in the title of this song, its lyrics are in dialect, without the words *nigga* or *darkey*. Unlike his previous minstrel songs, "The Glendy Burk" does not have a Southern setting. Rather, its main character is working in a northern hay field as he yearns for an idealized Southern world "wha dey work wid de sugar and de cane and roll on de cotton bale." Therefore, perhaps for the first time, Foster wrote about a freedman, albeit one who would risk his freedom to return to the South.

This song's title is taken from the name of an actual steamboat—the *Glenn D. Burke,* named for a New Orleans politician and businessman. In 1860, Foster's evocation of a big riverboat would have touched a chord of nostalgia in peo-

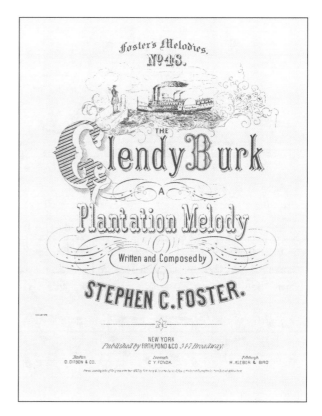

ple who had either never seen such a craft or had seen them supplanted by the railroads.

The Glendy Burk has a "funny old crew, and dey sing de boatman's song." This may be a reference to an early minstrel tune by Dan Emmett, "De Boatman's Dance" (1843), which itself is nostalgic for the earlier days of the keelboats. All these folks dance along to a lively melody that accompanies a "light, streamlined dialect" (Emerson 1997, 255).

Although Mr. Foster gave it his best effort, "The Glendy Burk" joined the ranks of his other post-1853 minstrel songs. It did not find popularity.

The Glendy Burk
Stephen C. Foster

Arranged for minstrel banjo by Daniel Partner
from "Foster's Melodies No 48"
New York: Firth, Pond & Co., 547 Broadway, 1860

Tuning: d, A, D, F#, A

Sheet of Stephen Foster's manuscript paper with various lines of music from the 1850s. Sketched on it in pencil is a banjo noting the common minstrel tuning in the key of G. *Foster Hall Collection, Center for American Music, University of Pittsburgh Library System.*

DON'T BET YOUR MONEY ON DE SHANGHAI
THE LAST MINSTREL SONG

In 1861, Mr. Foster wrote his last minstrel song, though it was not a success for him in terms of sales. In *Don't Bet Your Money On De Shanghai*, he returns to Negro dialect in the voice of a slave giving counsel about a cockfight wager. The jaunty melody and whimsical lyrics hearken back to Foster's early minstrel works, but what proved popular then could not revive Foster's career as war clouds gathered in the land. He doesn't include many of the popular minstrel elements that he used in former songs such as a plantation setting and idealized slave characters. So, this song may not have appealed to the audience's nostalgia.

Like many of the minstrels' songs, this one is a series of jokes. Even the freakish birds of the sideshow in verse two have to laugh at the Shanghai chicken with an odd crowing voice and insatiable appetite. Presumably, he is in no shape for fighting hence the advice: "Don't bet your money on de Shanghai."

The premise of this song is humorous because patrons of cockfighting would certainly know better than to bet on a Shanghai. Chickens of this breed, now called Cochin, created a sensation in England when they arrived from China as gifts to Queen Victoria. Introduced from England to America in 1845 and primarily bred for exhibition, Shanghai chickens were buff-colored and remarkable in appearance because of their great size and profuse soft feathering. This distinguished them from all other breeds at the time.

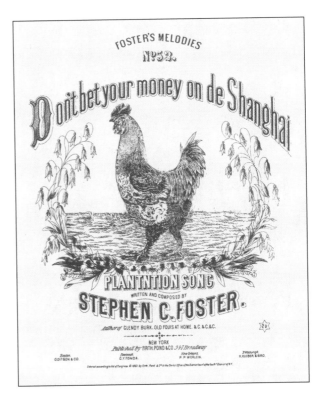

Stephen Foster previously wrote with flair of the changes that were occurring in his world. This is best observed in the seldom-heard second verse of "Oh! Susanna." But here, at the threshold of the Civil War, he does not allude to the convulsion that was about to overwhelm society nor does he attempt to feed the changing tastes of the American public.

Don't Bet Your Money On De Shanghai

Stephen C. Foster

Arranged for minstrel banjo by Daniel Partner
from "Foster's Melodies Np. 52"
New York: Firth, Pond & Co., 547 Broadway, 1861

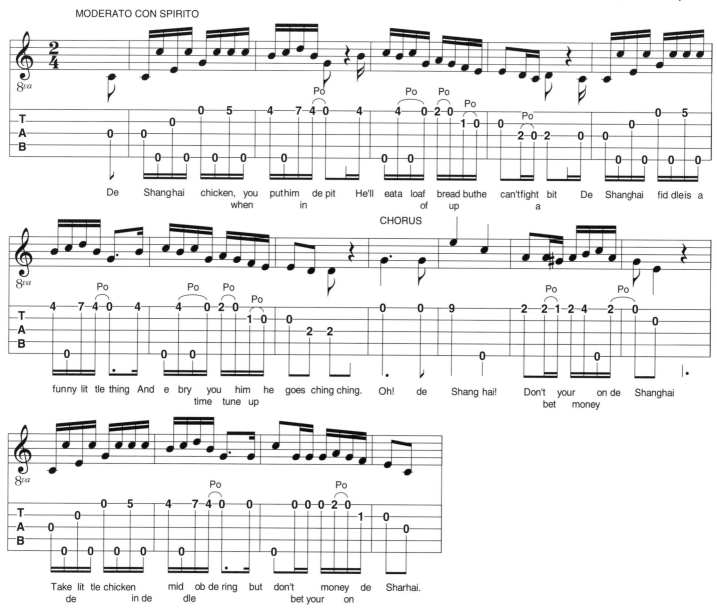

Tuning: d, A, D, F#, A

COMPLETE LYRICS

These lyrics conform to those published in their earliest sheet music editions. Most were written in a dialect that Stephen Foster, his fellow songwriters, and antebellum performers derived from the patois of American slaves. They also use slang common to that era. We have endeavored to retain the dialect, language, punctuation, and spelling of these lyrics as they appear in the earliest sheet music editions, even though today these may seem peculiar, in bad taste, or even extremely offensive. We think that accurate lyrics enable performers and audiences to better understand a song's meaning and historical milieu.

OH! SUSANNA (1848)

I come from Alabama
  with my Banjo on my knee
I'se gwine to Lou'siana
  My true lub for to see,
It rain'd all night de day I left,
  De wedder it was dry;
The sun so hot I froze to def;
  Susanna, dont you cry.

Oh! Susanna, do not cry for me,
I come from Alabama,
Wid my Banjo on my knee.

I jump'd aboard the telegraph
  and trabbled down de ribber,
De lectrick fluid magnified,
  and kill'd five hundred Nigga.
De bulgine bust and de hoss ran off,
  I really thought I'd die;
I shut my eyes to hold my bref
  Susanna dont you cry.

I had a dream de udder night,
  when ebry ting was still;
I thought I saw Susanna dear,
  a coming down de hill,
De buckwheat cake was in her mouf,
  de tear was in her eye,
I says, I'se coming from de souf,
  Susanna don't you cry.

WAY DOWN SOUF (1848)

We'll put for de souf Ah! dat's the place,
For the steeple chase
  and de bully hoss race—
Poker, brag, eucher, seven up and loo,
Den chime in Niggas,
  wont you come along too.

No use talkin when de
  Nigga wants to go,
Whar de corntop blossom
  and de canebrake grow;
Den come along to Cuba,
  and we'll dance de polka-juba,
Way down souf, whar de corn grow.

My lub she hab a very large mouf,
One corner in de norf,
  tudder corner in de souf;
It am so long, it reach so far—
Trabble all around it on a railroad car.

I went last night to see my Sally—
Two story house in Pigtail ally,
Whar de skeeters buz, fleas dey bite,
And de bull dogs howl
  and de tom cats fight.

MY BRODDER GUM (1849)

White folks I'll sing for you,
    Nuffin else to do,
Spend my time a pickin on de banjo,
    Hay! Brodder Gum.

My Brodder Gum,
    My Brodder Gum so fair,
    All de yaller galls runnin round,
    Try to get a lock ob his hair.

Hard work all de day,
    Hab no time to play
Berry fine time a diggin in the cornfield,
    Hay! Brudder Gum.

Tudder afternoon,
    I thought I saw de moon,
Saw my true lub comin through
    de cane-brake,
    Hay! Brudder Gum.

Went one berry fine day,
    To ride in a one horse sleigh,
Hollow'd to de old hoss
    comin through de tollgate,
    Hay! Brudder Gum.

OH! LEMUEL! (1850)

Oh! Lemuel my lark,
Oh Lemuel my beau,
I's guine to gib a ball to night,
I'd hab you for to know;
But if you want to dance,
Just dance outside de door;
Becayse your feet so berry large
Dey'll cover all de floor.

Oh! Lem! Lem! Lem! Lemuel I say!
Go down to de cotton field,
And bring de boys away.

Go down to de cotton field!
Go down, I say!
Go down and call de Nigga boys all:
We'll work no more to day. (x2)

Oh! Lemuel my hope,
Oh! Lemuel my joy
I'll tell you who'll be at de ball
My woolly headed boy.
Dere's Nelly Bly, you know,
And Juliana Snow,
Dere's cane-brake Kitty likes de boys,
And she'll be sure to go.

Oh! Lemuel is tall,
Oh! Lemuel is fair,
Oh Lemuel has gone to day
To take de morning air.
He makes de fiddle hum,
He makes de banjo tum,
He rattles on de old jaw bone,
And beats upon de drum.

NELLY BLY (1850)

Nelly Bly! Nelly Bly!
    bring de broom along,
We'll sweep de kitchen clean, my dear,
    and hab a little song.
Poke de wood, my lady lub,
    And make de fire burn,
And while I take de banjo down,
    Just gib de mush a turn.

Heigh! Nelly, Ho! Nelly,
    listen lub to me,
I'll sing for you play for you,
    a dulcem melody.
Heigh! Nelly, Ho! Nelly,
    listen lub, to me,
I'll sing for you, play for you
    a dulcem melody.

Nelly Bly hab a voice
    like de turtle dove,
I hears it in de meadow
    and I hears it in de grove
Nelly Bly hab a heart
    warm as cup ob tea,
And bigger dan de sweet potato
    down in Tennessee.

Nelly Bly shuts her eye
    when she goes to sleep,
When she wakens up again
    her eye-balls gin to peep
De way she walks, she lifts her foot,
    and den she brings it down,
And when it lights der's music dah
    in dat part ob de town.

Nelly Bly! Nelly Bly!
    nebber, nebber sigh,
Nebber bring de tear-drop
    to de corner ob your eye,
For de pie is made ob punkins
    and de mush is made of corn,
And der's corn and punkins plenty lub
    a lyin in de barn.

Gwine To Run All Night/ De Camptown Races (1850)

De Camptown ladies sing dis song
    Doodah! doodah!
De Camptown racetrack five miles long
    Oh! doodah day!
I come down dah wid my hat caved in
    Doodah! doodah!
I go back home wid a pocket full of tin
    Oh! doodah day!

Gwine to run all night!
Gwine to run all day!
I'll bet my money on de bobtail nag
Somebody bet on de bay.

De long tail filly and de big black hoss
    Doodah! doodah!
Dey fly de track and dey both cut across
    Oh! doodah day!
De blind hoss sticken in a big mud hole
    Doodah! doodah!
Can't touch bottom wid a ten foot pole
    Oh! doodah day!

Old muley cow come on to de track
    Doodah! doodah!
De bob-tail fling her ober his back
    Oh! doodah day!
Den fly along like a rail-road car
    Doodah! doodah!
Runnin' a race wid a shootin' star
    Oh! doodah day!

See dem flyin' on a ten mile heat
    Doodah! doodah!
Round de race track, den repeat
    Oh! doodah day!
I win my money on de bob-tail nag
    Doodah! doodah!
I keep my money in an old towbag
    Oh! doodah day!

Angelina Baker (1850)

Way down on de old plantation
    Dah's where I was born,
I used to beat de whole creation
    Hoein' in de corn:
Oh! den I work and den I sing
    So happy all de day,
Till Angelina Baker came
    And stole my heart away.

    Angelina Baker!
    Angelina Baker's gone
    She left me here to weep a tear
    And beat on de old jawbone.

I've seen my Angelina
    In de springtime and de fall,
I've seen her in de cornfield
    And I've seen her at de ball;
And ebry time I met her
    She was smiling like de sun,
But now I'm left to weep a tear
    Cayse Angelina's gone.

Angelina am so tall
    She nebber sees de ground,
She hab to take a wellumscope
    To look down on de town
Angelina likes de boys
    As far as she can see dem,
She used to run old Massa round
    To ax him for to free dem.

Early in de morning
    Ob a lubly summer day
I ax for Angelina,
    And dey say "she's gone away" —
I don't know wha to find her,
    Cayse I don't know wha she's gone,
She left me hear to weep a tear
    And beat on de old jawbone.

Way Down in Ca-i-ro (1850)

Oh! ladies dont you blush
    when I come out to play;
I only mean to please you all,
    and den I's guine away.

I hear my true-lub weep,
I hear my true-lub sigh,
'Way down in Ca-i-ro
    dis nigga's guine to die.

Sometimes de nigga's life is sad,
    sometimes his life is gay,
When de work dont come too hard
    he's singin all de day.

Now we libs on de fat ob de land,
    now we libs on de lean
When we hab no cake to bake
    we sweep de kitchen clean.

Massa bought a bran new coat
    and hung it on de wall,
Dis nigga's guine to take dat coat,
    and wear it to de ball.

All de ladies in de land,
    and all de gemmen too,
Am guine to hear de darkey band
    and see what dey can do.

Ring, Ring de Banjo! (1851)

De time is nebber dreary
   If de darkey nebber groans;
De ladies nebber weary
   Wid de rattle ob de bones:
Den come again Susanna
   By de gaslight ob de moon;
We'll tum de old Piano
   When de banjo's out ob tune.

   Ring, ring de banjo!
   I like dat good old song,
   Come again my true lub,
   Oh! wha you been so long.

Oh! Nebber count de bubbles
   While der's water in de spring:
De darkey hab no troubles
   While he's got dis song to sing.
De beauties of creation
   Will nebber lose der charm
While I roam de old plantation
   Wid my true lub on my arm.

Once I was so lucky,
   My massa set me free,
I went to old Kentucky
   To see what I could see:
I could not go no farder,
   I turn to massa's door,
I lub him all de harder,
   I'll go away no more.

Early in de morning
   Ob a lubly summer day,
My massa send me warning
   He'd like to hear me play.
On de banjo tapping,
   I come wid dulcem strain;
Massa fall a napping
   He'll nebber wake again.

My lub, I'll hab to leabe you
   While de ribber's running high;
But I nebber can deceibe you
   So dont you wipe your eye.
I's guine to make some money;
   But I'll come anodder day
I'll come again my honey,
   If I hab to work my way.

Oh! Boys, Carry Me 'Long (1851)

Oh! carry me 'long;
   Der's no more trouble for me:
I's guine to roam In a happy home
   Where all de niggas are free.
I've worked long in de fields;
   I've handled many a hoe:
I'll turn my eye, Before I die,
   And see de sugarcane grow.

Oh! boys, carry me 'long;
Carry me till I die
Carry me down
To de buryin' groun'
Massa, dont you cry;

All ober de land
   I've wandered many a day,
To blow de horn And mind de corn
   And Keep de possum away.
No use for me now
   So darkeys bury me low:
My horn is dry, And I must lie
   Wha de possum nebber can go.

Farewell to de boys
   Wid hearts so happy and light,
Dey sing a song De whole day long,
   And dance de juba at night;
Farewell to de fields
   Ob cotton, 'bacco, and all:
I's guine to hoe in a bressed row
   Wha de corn grows mellow and tall.

Farewell to de hills,
   De meadows covered wid green,
Old brindle Boss And de old grey hoss
   All beaten, broken, and lean.
Farewell to de dog
   Dat always followed me 'round;
Old Sancho'll wail And droop his tail
   When I am under de ground.

Old Folks at Home (1851)

Way down upon de Swanee ribber,
   Far, far away,
Dere's whar my heart is turning ebber,
   Dere's whar de old folks stay.
All up and down de whole creation,
   Sadly I roam,
Still longing for de old plantation,
   And for de old folks at home.

All de world am sad and dreary,
   Eb'ry where I roam;
Oh! darkeys, how my heart
   grows weary,
Far from de old folks at home.

All round de little farm I wander'd
   When I was young,
Den many happy days I squander'd,
   Many de songs I sung.
When I was playing wid my brudder
   Happy was I.
Oh! take me to my kind old mudder,
   Dere let me live and die.

One little hut among de bushes,
   One dat I love,
Still sadly to my mem'ry rushes,
   No matter where I rove
When will I see de bees a humming
   All round de comb?
When will I hear de banjo tumming,
   Down in my good old home?

Massa's in de Cold Ground (1852)

Round de meadows am a ringing
   De darkeys' mournful song,
While de mocking-bird am singing,
   Happy as de day am long.
Where de ivy am a creeping
   O'er de grassy mound,
Dare old massa am a sleeping,
   Sleeping in de cold, cold ground.

Down in de cornfield
Hear dat mournful sound:
All de darkeys am a weeping
Massa's in de cold, cold ground.

When de autumn leaves were falling,
   When de days were cold,
'Twas hard to hear old massa calling,
   Cayse he was so weak and old.
Now de orange tree am blooming
   On de sandy shore,
Now de summer days am coming,
   Massa nebber calls no more.

Massa made de darkeys love him,
   Cayse he was so kind,
Now dey sadly weep above him,
   Mourning cayse he leave dem behind.
I cannot work before tomorrow,
   Cayse de tear drops flow,

I try to drive away my sorrow
   Pickin on de old banjo.

My Old Kentucky Home, Good-Night! (1853)

The sun shines bright in the
   old Kentucky home,
'Tis summer, the darkies are gay,
The corn top's ripe and the meadow's
   in the bloom
While the birds make music all the day.
The young folks roll on the
   little cabin floor,
All merry, all happy and bright:
By'n by Hard Times comes a knocking
   at the door,
Then my old Kentucky Home, good night!

Weep no more, my lady,
   oh! weep no more today!
We will sing one song
For the old Kentucky Home,
For the old Kentucky Home,
   far away.

They hunt no more for the possum
   and the coon
On the meadow, the hill and the shore,
They sing no more by the glimmer
   of the moon,
On the bench by the old cabin door.
The day goes by like a shadow
   O're the heart,
With sorrow where all was delight:
The time has come when the darkies
   have to part,
Then my old Kentucky Home,
   good-night!

The head must bow and the back
   will have to bend,
Wherever the darkey may go:
A few more days, and the trouble
   all will end
In the field where the sugar-canes grow.
A few more days for to tote
   the weary load,
No matter, 'twill never be light,
A few more days till we
   totter on the road,
Then my old Kentucky Home,
   good-night!

THE GLENDY BURK (1860)

De Glendy Burk is a mighty fast boat,
   Wid a mighty fast captain too;
He sits up dah on de hurricane roof
   And he keeps his eye on de crew.
I cant stay here, for dey work too hard;
   I'm bound to leave dis town;
I'll take my duds and tote 'em on my back
   When de Glendy Burk comes down.

   Ho! for Lou'siana!
   I'm bound to leave dis town;
   I'll take my duds and
      tote 'em on my back
   When de Glendy Burk comes down.

De Glendy Burk has a funny old crew
   And dey sing de boatman's song,
Dey burn de pitch and de pine knot too,
   For to shove de boat along.
De smoke goes up and de ingine roars
   And de wheel goes round and round,
So fair you well! for I'll take a little ride
   When de Glendy Burk comes down.

I'll work all night in de wind and storm,
   I'll work all day in de rain,
Till I find myself on de levydock
   In New Orleans again.
Dey make me mow in de hay field here
   And knock my head wid de flail,
I'll go wha dey work wid de sugar
   and de cane
And roll on de cotton bale.

My lady love is as pretty as a pink,
   I'll meet her on de way
I'll take her back to de sunny old south
   And dah I'll make her stay
So dont you fret my honey dear,
   Oh! dont you fret Miss Brown
I'll take you back 'fore de
   middle of de week
   When de Glendy Burk comes down.

DON'T BET YOUR MONEY ON DE SHANGHAI (1861)

De Shanghai chicken,
   when you put him in de pit,
He'll eat a loaf of bread up,
   but he can't fight a bit
De Shanghai fiddle is a funny little thing
And ebry time you tune him up
   he goes ching ching.

Oh! de Shanghai!
Don't bet your money on de Shanghai!
Take de little chicken
   in de middle ob de ring
But don't bet your money on de Shanghai.

I go to de fair for to see
   de funny fowls
De double headed pigion
   an de one eyed owls
De old lame goose wid
   no web between his toes
He kills himself a laughing
   when de Shanghai crows.

De Shanghai's tall but his
   appetite is small
He'll only swallow ebry thing
   that he can overhaul
Four bags of wheat just as
   certain as your born
A bushel of potatoes and a
   tub full of corn.

WORKS CITED

Austin, William W. *Susanna, Jeannie, and the Old Folks At Home.* New York: Macmillan Publishing Co., 1975.

Bean, Annemarie et al. *Inside the Minstrel Mask.* Hanover: University Press of New England [for] Wesleyan University Press, 1996.

Briggs, Thomas. *Briggs Banjo Instructor of 1855.* Bremo Bluff, VA: Tuckahoe Music, 1992.

Brighton, Terry. *Hell Riders.* New York: Henry Holt, 2004.

Cockrell, Dale. *Demons of Disorder.* Cambridge: Cambridge University Press, 1997.

Emerson, Ken. *Doo-Dah!.* New York: Simon & Schuster, 1997.

Gura, Phillip F., and James F. Bollman. *America's Instrument.* Chapel Hill: The University of North Carolina Press, 1999.

Howard, John Tasker. *Stephen Foster, America's Troubadour.* New York: T. Y. Crowell Co., 1962.

Lawrence, Vera Brodsky. *Strong on Music, Volume 2.* Chicago: The University of Chicago Press, 1995.

Linn, Karen. *That Half-Barbaric Twang.* Chicago, University of Illinois Press, 1994.

Lott, Eric. *Love and Theft.* New York: Oxford University Press, 1995.

Mahar, William J. *Behind the Burnt Cork Mask.* Chicago: University of Chicago Press, 1999.

Morneweck, Evelyn Foster. *Chronicles of Stephen Foster's Family, Volume I.* Pittsburgh: University of Pittsburgh Press, 1944.

Morneweck, Evelyn Foster. *Chronicles of Stephen Foster's Family, Volume II.* Pittsburgh: University of Pittsburgh Press, 1944.

Morrison Foster. *My Brother Stephen.* Indianapolis: Privately Printed, 1932.

Nathan, Hans. *Dan Emmett and the Rise of Early Negro Minstrelsy.* Norman: University of Oklahoma Press, 1962.

Sacks, Howard, and Judith Rose Sacks. *Way up North in Dixie.* Washington: Smithsonian Institution Press, 1993.

Saunders, Steven and Deane L. Root. *The Music of Stephen C. Foster, Volume 1, 1844–1855.* Washington: Smithsonian Institution Press, 1990.

Szego, Peter and George Wunderluch. "Art and Craft of the Early Banjo." In *The Birth of the Banjo.* Katonah: Katonah Museum of Art, 2003.

Toll, Robert C. *Blacking Up.* New York: Oxford University Press, 1974.

Winans Robert B. and Elias J. Kaufman. "Minstrel and Classic Banjo: American and English Connections." *American Music* 12 (1994): 11.

Wittke, Carl. *Tambo and Bones.* Westport: Greenwood Press, 1968.

ABOUT THE AUTHORS

Edwin J. Sims is an avid student of antebellum popular and military history. His primary focus is on music, photography and equestrianism.

Daniel Partner is a writer, book editor, and musician, and lives with his wife, Margaret, on the south Oregon coast.

Readers can write to the authors at banjoknee@gmail.com.

More Great Banjo Books from Centerstream...